Brad Benedict

Indigo Books NEW YORK

The Imperial Presidency Mick Haggerty

Elvis Cynthia Marsh

Campbell's Soup Can 1964 Andy Warhol

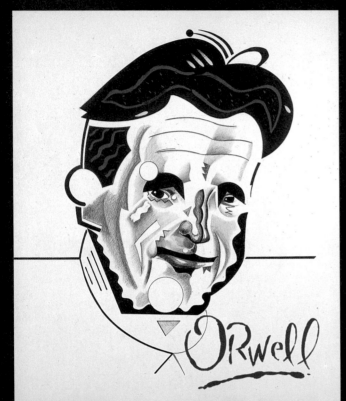

George Orwell Clive Piercy

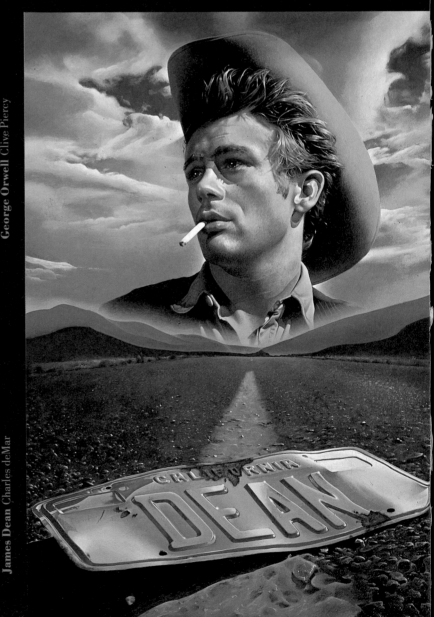

James Dean Charles deMar

Inquiries should be addressed to Indigo Books, 724 Fifth Avenue, New York, New York 10019.

U.S. AND CANADIAN BOOK DISTRIBUTION:
Grove Press, Inc.
196 West Houston Street
New York, New York 10014

OVERSEAS BOOK DISTRIBUTION:
Indigo Books, an imprint of American Showcase, Inc.
724 Fifth Avenue
New York, New York 10019
Tel: 212-245-0981

Printed in Japan

First Printing

ISBN: 0-394-62303-7

Library of Congress
Catalogue Card No. 84-80884

FOREWORD

When Brad Benedict asked me to write a foreword
to his second edition of FAME, he suggested that
I address myself to the two subjects with which his
book is concerned: celebrity and illustration. And so
I will. But first a little something about Brad.

Brad Benedict was born during the Fifties, in the
height of summer and the flats of Beverly Hills,
which he remembers as a place dominated by price
wars and civil strife. He spent his formative
years happily ensconced in front of the family
Zenith, where he fell hopelessly in love with the
icons of the age—Lucy, Looney Tunes and Joi
Lansing, to name his top three. Many of his
generation have managed to make the leap from Porky
Pig to Fine Art. Not Brad. No amount of peer pressure
could diminish his ardor for the indelible images
of his childhood. To this day, Max Fleischer is
his Van Gogh; and Gumby, his Venus de Milo.

And I am with him every step of the way!

Oh, Brad! What a doll you are—to be such a
gallant defender of popular art in times as pompous
as these!

I will never forget the afternoon I committed the
monumental gaucherie of announcing over a brunch
in Soho that Maxfield Parrish was my favorite
artist. Shut up and shut out, I was forced to flee
the bistro, roundly pelted every step of the way
by chunks of raw fish and cold pasta.

But let them pelt and let them pummel. The illustra-
tions in this book are vivid proof that lovers of
<u>arte populaire</u> need not hide their heads in shame.
I don't intend to. Why should you?

Instead, thrill to it all—Boy George as the Mona
Lisa! Julia Child murdering a salad! Sophia Loren
as Sophia Duck! Sue Mengers' nails gleaming like
knives! Ronald Reagan dropping The Big One!
Everyone you love and everyone you love to hate are
captured for eternity in these colorful pages. From Fred
Astaire to Pia Zadora, you'll find them all here
in striking, unforgettable images strewn about with
sumptuous abandon.

All this and more you hold in your hands. Turn the
page and you'll discover the most astounding col-
lection of contemporary illustration since Brad
compiled FAME I.

Thanks, Brad.

—**Bette Midler**
May 15, 1984

Bette Midler Richard Bernstein

Laverne and Shirley Richard Amsel
Faye Dunaway and Jack Nicholson Richard Amsel

Ronnie and Nancy Robert Risko
Tracy and Hepburn James Henry

Rick Springfield Cynthia Marsh
Liza and Chita Robert Risko

Carmen Miranda and Groucho Kirsten Soderlind
Liz and Dick Robert Risko
Mick and Keith Katsu

Twiggy and Tommy Tune Robert Risko
Rod Stewart Everett Peck

Tess Harper and Robert Duvall Paul Tankersley
Hall and Oates Robert Risko
Jacqueline Bisset Kim Whitesides

6

Bobby Kennedy Roy Lichtenstein

J.F.K. Marvin Mattelson ➤

Duke Ellington Pearl Beach

Louis Armstrong Hovik Dilakian

Dizzy Gillespie Katsu

Duke Ellington Laura Smith

LAURA SMITH

Al Jarreau Rich Mahon

Quincy Jones Stan Watts

Count Basie Cynthia Marsh

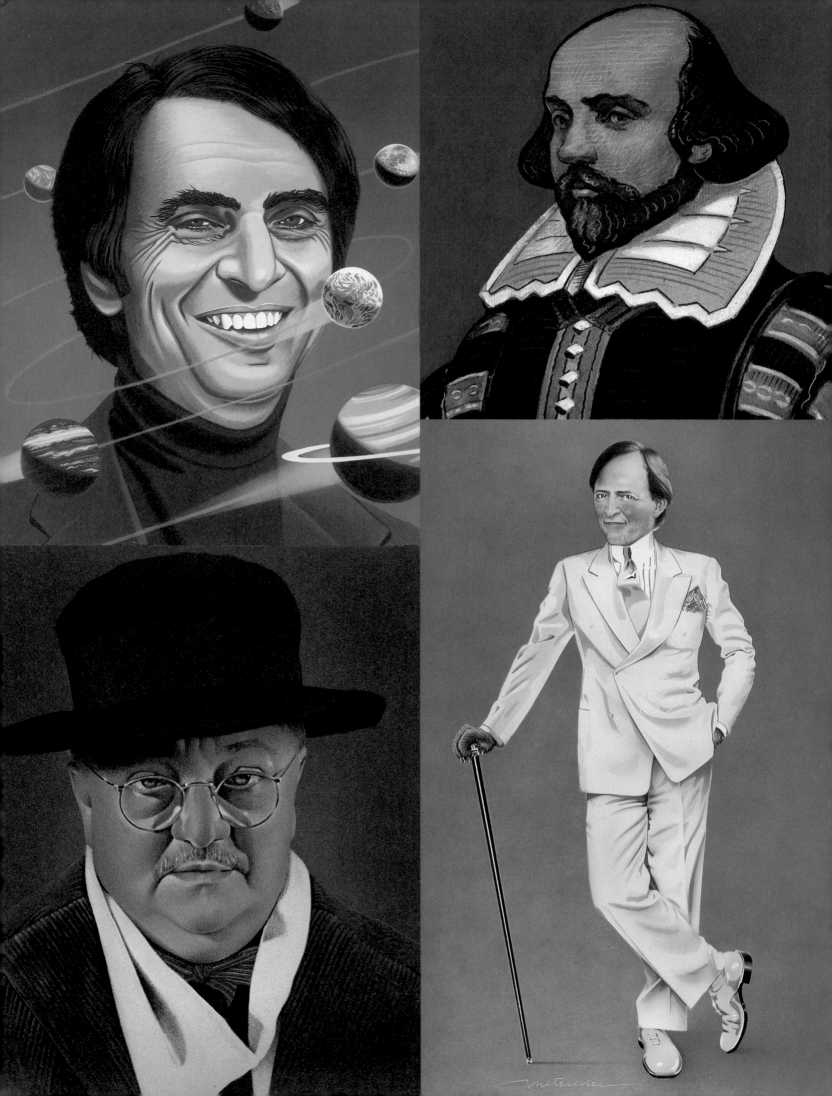

Warhol Regina Argentin   **Louise Nevelson** Marvin Mattelson

Carl Sagan Paul Reott
Alexander Woollcott Kirsten Soderlind

Shakespeare George Masi
Tom Wolfe Kim Whitesides

David Hockney Kyoko Tsuchihashi

Bette Davis Bernard Bonhomme

Goldie Hawn Robert Risko

Rita Hayworth Tom Edinger

Jayne Mansfield Gary Panter

Carole Lombard Raphaelle Goethals

Meryl Streep Mick Haggerty

Harlow Tom Edinger

Greta Garbo Ken Konno

14

The Rolling Stones Katsu
Jackson Browne Katsu
Bob Dylan Katsu
Patti Smith Katsu

David Bowie Katsu
Mick Jones (Clash) Katsu
Keith Richards Katsu

Willie Nelson Katsu
Jim Morrison Katsu
Iggy Pop Katsu

15

Laurie Anderson Cathy Barancik

Richard Pryor Kathy Staico Schorr

John Cleese Malcolm Harrison

Buck Henry David Willardson

Mia Farrow Harumi Yamaguchi

Woody Allen Robert Risko

18

Joan Collins Michael K. Conway

Norman Mailer I Mick Haggerty

Duckula Neon Park

Jack Benny Cynthia Marsh, Mike Doud

Boy George Kyoxo Tsuchihashi

Doris Day Kari Bravman

Divine Richard Bernstein

Sinatra Mick Haggerty

The **BeeGees** Kim Whitesides
The Police Lou Beach

Crosby, Stills and Nash Robert Grossman
The Beatles Tadanori Yokoo

Y M O   Yosuke Kawamura

The Police Mick Haggerty

Muhammad Ali Jeff Gold ➤

Reggie Jackson Robert Risko

Earl Weaver Marvin Mattelson

Bruce Jenner Robert Grossman

Sugar Ray Leonard Lou Brooks

Tommy Lasorda Kim Whitesides

Jimmy Connors Robert Grossman

MANDreLL
Sisters

Lee   BARbRA   Bell

PRetty LAdies

NANCY KI...   Betsy BloomingdALe   ChArlene TILton
NANcy Reagan

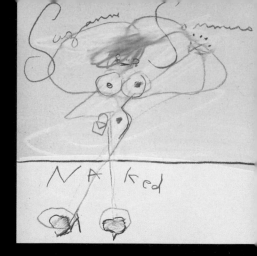

Suzanne Sommers

NAked

BArbrA STEISAND

Yentel Soup

Ladie Authours

Jackie Collins   "U" Judith Krantz

DYNASTY

HELP

Peoples Court

Judge Wopner

Doug Lon Elle

Mr. Jones   Leona Hemsley

CASE OF THE Poodle Puddles

The Boone FAMILY

PAT Mrs. Boone   Jan Cindy Cherry Debby

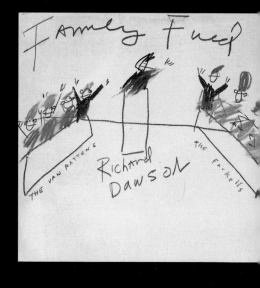

Family Feud

THE VAN PATTONS   Richard Dawson   THE Forkells

S T A S

..NN   JILLIAN   LyndA Carter Loni ANderson

LAte Night

DAVID LettermAn

Dr. Ruth WESTHimer

Celebrity Squares Cathy Baranick

Julia Child Robert Grossman ▶

26 **Elvis** Cynthia Marsh   **Nina Hagen** Nick Taggart
Grace Jones Nick Taggart   **Jagger** Cynthia Marsh

27 **Lennon** Cynthia Marsh   **Annie Lennox** Nick Taggart
Chrissie Hynde Nick Taggart   **Sting** Cynthia Marsh

Mel Brooks Bush Hollyhead

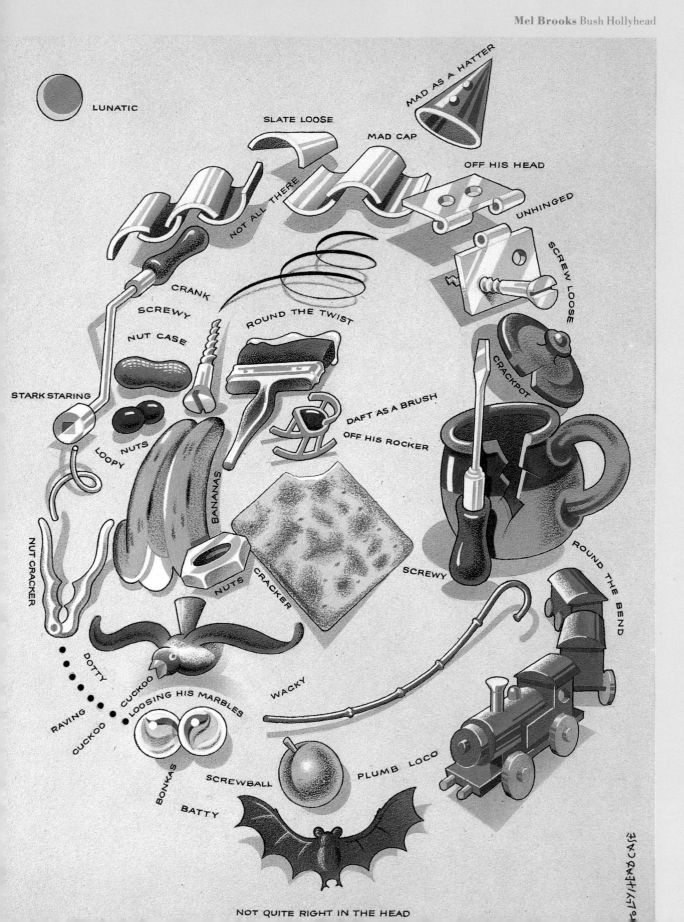

NOT QUITE RIGHT IN THE HEAD

Awesome Welles Ed Wexler

Jerry Lewis Todd Schorr

Lily Tomlin Richard Amsel

Annie Lennox Kyoko Tsuchihashi

Go-Go's Cynthia Marsh

Nina Hagen Katsu

Blondie Kim Whitesides

Annabella (Bow Wow Wow) Conny Jude

Exene (X) Craig Shannon

Rickie Lee Jones Rich Mahon

Mr. "T" Gary Panter

◀ Godzilla Todd Schorr

King Kong Robert Kopecky

Rodney Dangerfield Craig Shannon

Natalie Wood

Burt Reynolds

Ann-Margret

Robert Redford

Jayne Mansfield

Kris Kristofferson

Jacqueline Bisset

Dolly Parton Mark Weatherhead

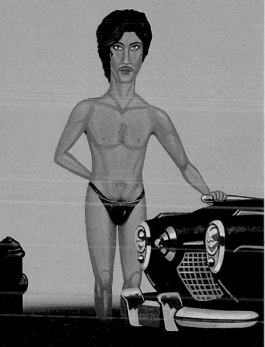

Doris Day

Stevie Winwood

Todd Rundgren

Paul McCartney

Prince

Ry Cooder

Jimmy Cliff

Bobby "Blue" Bland

Yosuke Kawamura

Pete Townshend Jim Salvati

Sting and Stewart Pearl Beach

Billy Joel Kim Whitesides

Boy George Cathy Barancik

My Name is NEIL YOUNG

who are you?

Neil Young Katsu

Tom Petty Patricia Dryden

Joe Jackson Yosuke Kawamura

Otis Redding Hiroshi Nagai

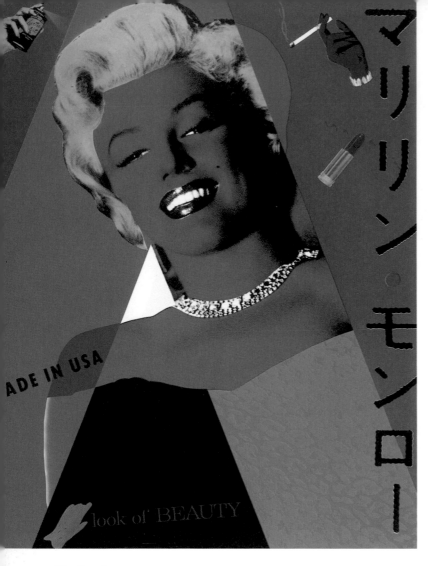

マリリン・モンロー

Marilyn Vartan

John Travolta Bush Hollyhead

David Bowie Laurie Rosenwald

38

Harrison Ford Kathy Staico Schorr
Bogart Tom Tomita

Robert Mitchum Pearl Beach
Clint Eastwood Richard Hernández

39

Warren Beatty Mick Haggerty

Julie ANDREWS

•AMSEL•

Walter MATTHAU

Little MISS MARKER

Tony ★ CURTIS ★ Bob ★ NEWHART ★ Lee ★ GRANT

AND INTRODUCING ★ Sara ★ STIMSON AS "LITTLE MISS MARKER"

Little Miss Marker Richard Amsel

Tom Waits Robert Risko

Miles Davis Katsu

Buddy Holly Bush Hollyhead

Frank Sinatra Kim Whitesides

George Clinton Craig Shannon

Elvis Costello Cathy Barancik

Gilda Radner Dennis Ziemienski

Katharine Hepburn Kim Whitesides
Kate Smith Paul Tankersley

Pia Zadora Ben Osto
Barbra Streisand Richard Amsel

Loni Anderson James Henry
Julia Child Robert Risko

Jane Fonda Robert Risko

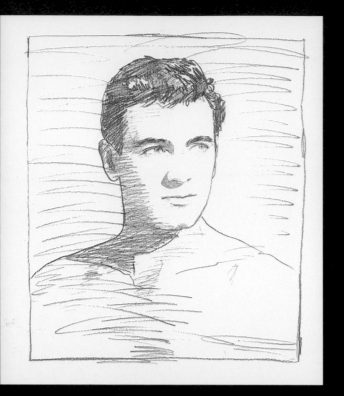

Rock Hudson Pater Sato

Lucy Pater Sato

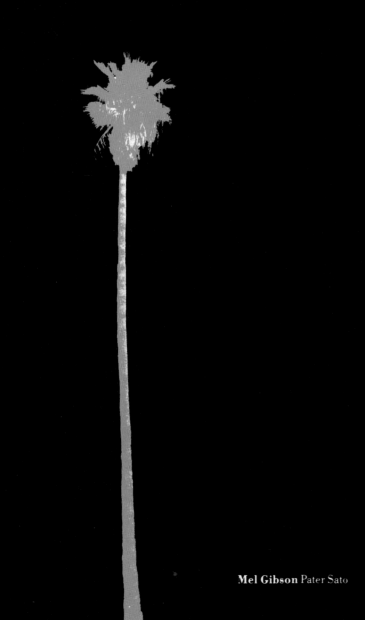

Mel Gibson Pater Sato

Charles Mingus Jeff Gold

Pee Wee Herman Gary Panter

Robin Williams Everett Peck

Groucho Ann Meisel

George Burns Robert Grossman

Andy Kaufman Ben Osto

Bob Hope Richard Amsel

Eddie Murphy Robert Kopecky

50
Jeremy Irons John Geary
Tom Selleck Richard Amsel

Dudley Moore Ann Meisel
Robert Duvall Kim Whitesides

51
Susan Sarandon Randy Glass
Liv Ullmann Robert Risko

Joan Collins Alan Daniels
Charlotte Rampling Harumi Yamaguchi

Wendy O Williams Richard Merkin ➤

The Oreos Ed Wexler

The B-52's Pater Sato ➤

Kid Creole and the Coconuts Katsu

Barbara Cartland Wendy Burden

Sam Shepard Robert Kopecky

Raymond Chandler Yosuke Kawamura

John Irving Marvin Mattelson

S.J. Perelman Richard Merkin

Henry Miller Katsu

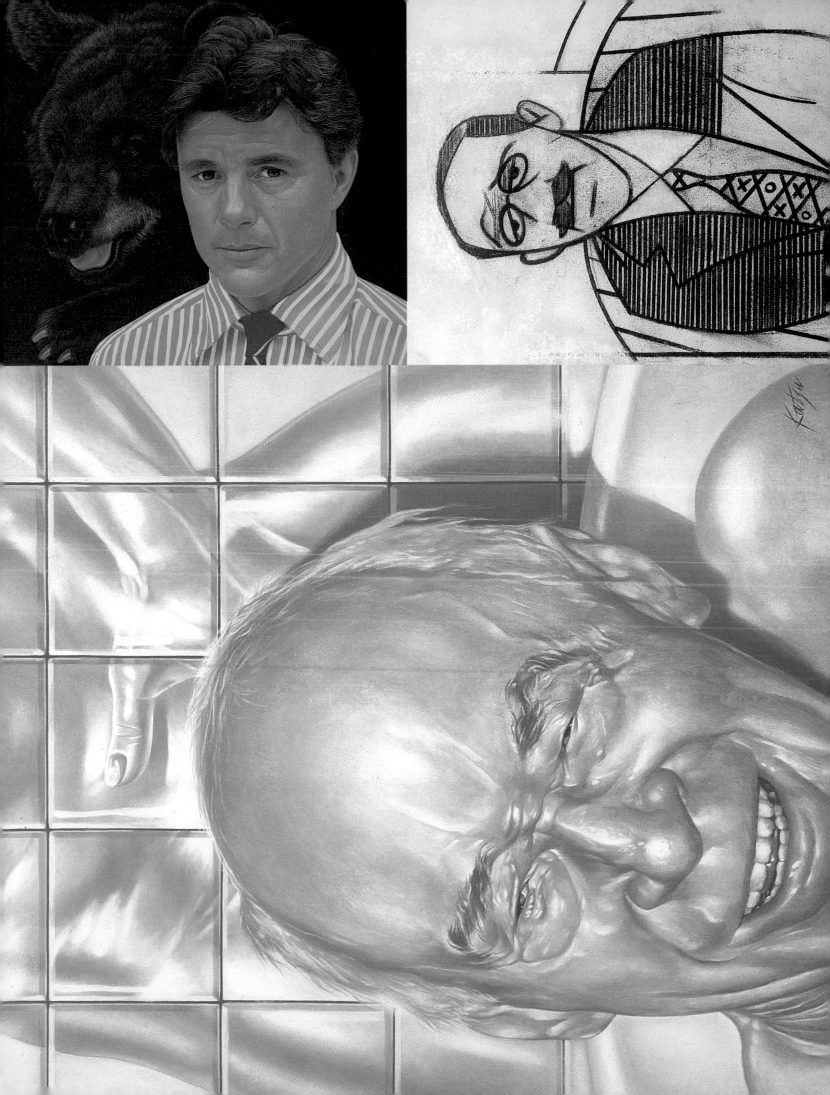

Adam Ant Regina Argentin

Ricky Schroder Cynthia Marsh

Warhol Katsu

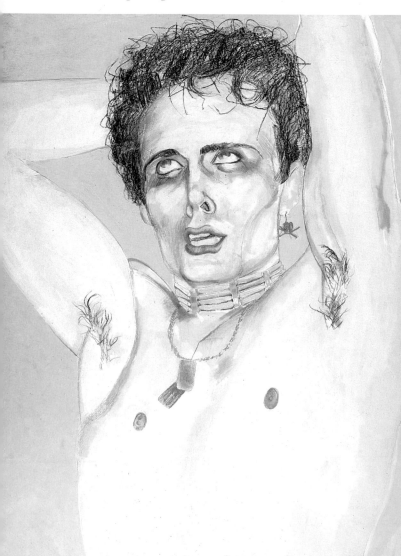

Albert Einstein Saul Bernstein

Elvis Robert Kopecky

Pee Wee Herman Robert Risko

Richard Dreyfuss Iku Akiyama

Tony Geary Ann Meisel

Gene Tierney

Elizabeth Taylor

Kim Novak

Grace Kelly

Ava Gardner

Katharine Hepburn Harumi Yamaguchi

Liza Minnelli

Truman Capote Andy Warhol

Mick Jagger

David Hockney

Andy Warhol Osamu Harada

Golda Meir

The Pop Boys Lou Brooks

62

Santa Claus Kim Whitesides
Heaven, Hell, and Rock & Roll Ben Osto

63

Dracula Gary Ruddell
Wolfman Gary Ruddell

Lauren Bacall Brian Zick

Buddy Holly
David Bowie
Stevie Wonder

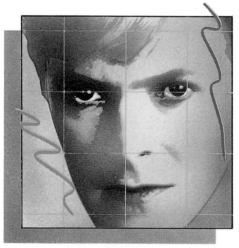

John Lennon
Aretha Franklin
Bruce Springsteen David Willardson

Elvis Presley
Mick Jagger
Deborah Harry

Rodney Bingenheimer Ed Wexler ➤

Jagger Ken Konno

Bowie

Dylan

Lennon

'Scuse me while I kiss the sky
Purple haze all in my eyes
You're

Jimi Hendrix Rob Wilson

Alan Freed Robert Burger

Luis Buñuel Ian Wright

Steven Spielberg Robert Grossman

'۱۸۳۱۶

Akira Buñuel Kurosawa Katsu

Woody Allen Everett Peck

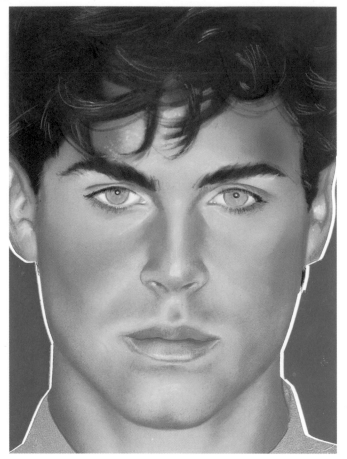

Rob Lowe Richard Bernstein

Nastassja Kinski Jeff Gold

Matt Dillon Ann Field

Brooke Shields Jeff Gold

Judy Garland Richard Amsel

Fred Astaire Tom Tomita

Liz Taylor Regina Argentin

Paul Newman Kim Whitesides

70

Gloria Swanson

Ann-Margret

Geoffrey Holder

Annette Funicello

Arnold Schwarzenegger

Joan Rivers

George Burns Robert Risko

Maria Callas Wendy Burden

Wally and "the Beaver" Rhonda Voo

J.F.K. and Nixon Robert Grossman

Dick Powell and Ruby Keeler Richard Amsel

Laurel and Hardy Robert Grossman

William Powell and Jean Harlow Mark Sparacio

Sunset Blvd. Nick Taggart

Marilyn Bette Levine

Marilyn 1962 Andy Warhol ➤

Marilyn Tara Yamura

74

Rod Stewart Malcolm Harrison
Rod Stewart Patricia Dryden

75

Mick Jagger Pam Wall
Mick Jagger Bette Levine

Marilyn Robert Risko

Marilyn Monroe Tadanori Yokoo

Brian Setzer (Stray Cats) Regina Argentin

Walter Cronkite Kirsten Soderlind

Sal Mineo Ann Meisel

Sue Mengers Robert Grossman

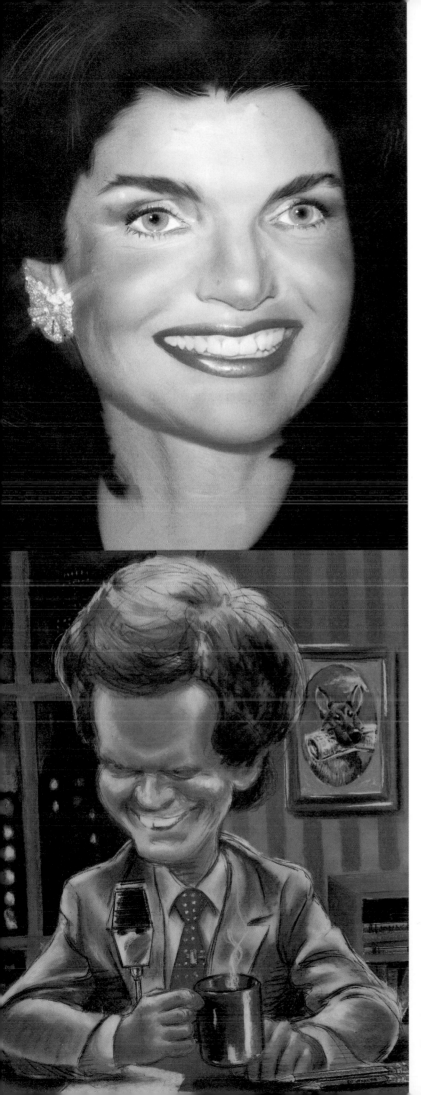

Jackie O. Richard Bernstein

Nathanael West Jim Heimann

David Letterman Ed Wexler

Giorgio Moroder Robert Risko

Young Elvis Lou Beach

Lou Reed Patricia Dryden

Bob Marley Bush Hollyhead

David Byrne Frank Olinsky

Bowie Laurie Rosenwald

Halston Andy Warhol

Y.S.L. Andy Warhol

Daniel Hechter Jim Cherry

Kenzo Ann Field

Diana Vreeland Wendy Burden

Richard Gere

Jodie Foster

Mariel Hemingway

Mick Jagger

Goldie Hawn

Calvin Klein Richard Bernstein

Joan Rivers Wendy Burden

Jane Fonda Ann Meisel

Esther Williams Regina Argentin

Sylvester Stallone Everett Peck

Bruce Lee Jeff Gold

Malcolm McDowell Katsu

86

David Bowie Katsu

87

Curtis Mayfield
Al Green

Sam Cooke
Joe Tex Hiroshi Nagai

Edie Sedgwick Regina Argentin

◄ **Our Gang** Paul Tankersley

Earl Scheib Kari Brayman

Ronnie Raygun Clive Piercy

◄ **Uncle Miltie** Tom Dolle

James Dean Gary Panter

Elvis David Willardson

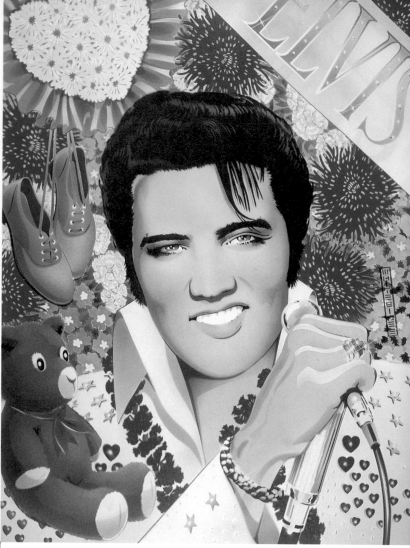

Elvis Kim Whitesides

Elvis Richard Amsel

Elvis Ron Lieberman ➤

Elvis Iku Akiyama

Margaret Trudeau Everett Peck

The Sixties Cynthia Marsh

Spago Nick Taggart

◄ **The Royal Family** Paul Cemmick

M∗A∗S∗H Stan Watts

Hank Williams Robert Burger

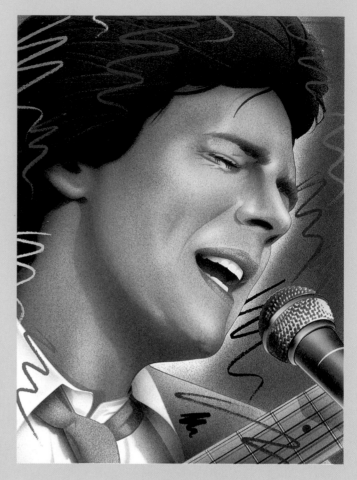

Rick Springfield David Willardson

Michael Jackson Pam Wall

Elton John Ann Meisel

Liberace Ann Meisel

Rick James Bernard Bonhomme

David Bowie Patrick James

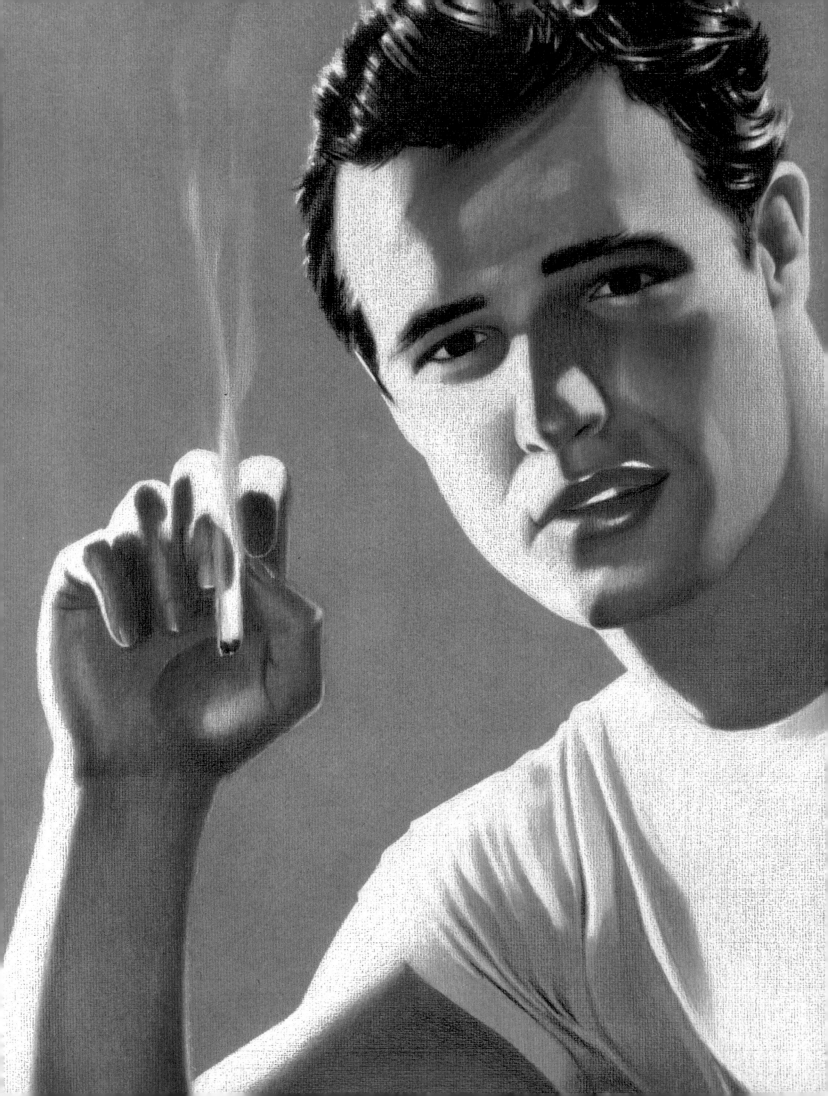

Ingrid Bergman

Brigitte Bardot

Maureen O'Hara Harumi Yamaguchi

Brando Tom Edinger

99

98   **Billy Idol** Kathy Staico Schorr

Sinatra Ben Osto
Lawrence Welk Cynthia Marsh

Pat Boone James Henry
Sammy Davis Jr. Mark Weatherhead

Reagan Ed Wexler

Reagan Robert Risko

Reagan Ben Osto

Reagan Ed Wexler

Ronnie Warbucks Robert Kopecky

Reagan Nigel Holmes

Diana Ross Robert Risko

Stevie Nicks Rich Mahon

Billie Holiday Rhonda Voo

Pearl Bailey Rhonda Voo

Joni Mitchell Barbara Nessim

Billie Holiday Mark Weatherhead

WEATHERHEAD

Freud Robert Grossman

Johnny Carson Marvin Mattelson

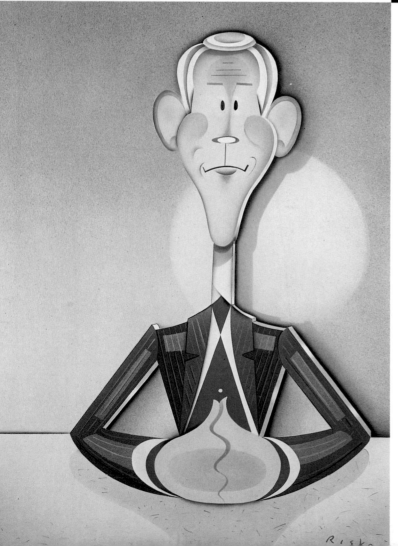

Johnny Carson Robert Risko

Johnny Carson Cynthia Marsh, Mike Doud ➤

Joan Rivers Stephen Kelemen

Mickey Mummy Everett Peck

Minkey Mouse Mike Fink

Queen Elizabeth Peter Knock

Yasir Arafat Craig Shannon

Leonid Brezhnev Craig Shannon

Mickey Mondrian Mick Haggerty

Chiang Ching (Mao's widow) Pearl Beach

Walt Disney Cynthia Marsh, Mike Doud

Ray Charles Hiroshi Nagai   **Peter Tosh** Jim Salvati

Bob Marley Yosuke Kawamura

James Brown Robert Grossman

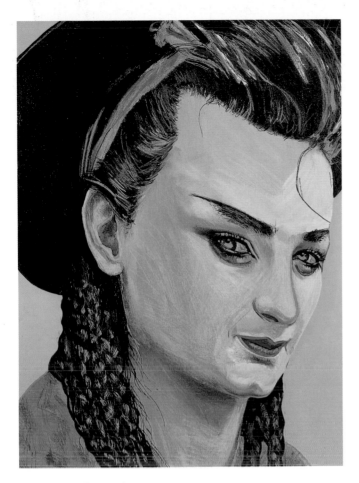

Boy George Regina Argentin

Keith Moon Bush Hollyhead

Bowie Craig Shannon

John Lennon Rob Wilson

WEATHERHEAD 78

Sophia Loren Mark Weatherhead

Sophia Duck Neon Park

Raquel Duck Neon Park
Raquel Welch Harumi Yamaguchi

Dietrich Ken Konno
Marlene Duck Neon Park

INDEX

Akiyama, Iku 57, 90
Ali, Muhammad 23
Allen, Woody 17, 67
Amsel, Richard 4, 29, 41, 45, 49, 50, 69, 72, 90
Anderson, Laurie 15
Anderson, Loni 45
Annabella 31
Ann-Margret 34, 70
Ant, Adam 56
Arafat, Yasir 107
Argentin, Regina 11, 56, 69, 78, 84, 88, 109
Armstrong, Louis 8
Astaire, Fred 69
B-52's, The 53
Bacall, Lauren 63
Bailey, Pearl 103
Ball, Lucille 46
Barancik, Cathy 15, 24, 36, 43
Bardot, Brigitte 97
Basie, Count 9
Beach, Lou 20, 80
Beach, Pearl 8, 36, 38, 107
Beatles, The 20
Beatty, Warren 39
Beaver and Wally 72
Bee Gees, The 20
Benny, Jack 18
Bergman, Ingrid 97
Berle, Milton 88
Bernstein, Richard 3, 19, 68, 79, 83
Bernstein, Saul 56
Bingenheimer, Rodney 65
Bisset, Jacqueline 5, 34
Bland, Bobby "Blue" 35
Blondie 31
Bogart, Humphrey 38
Bonhomme, Bernard 12, 95
Boone, Pat 98
Bowie, David 14, 40, 64, 65, 81, 86, 95, 109
Boy George 19, 36, 109
Brando, Marlon 96
Brayman, Kari 19, 89
Brezhnev, Leonid 107
Brooks, Lou 23, 53, 61
Brooks, Mel 28
Brown, James 108
Browne, Jackson 14
Buñuel, Luis 66
Burden, Wendy 54, 71, 82, 84
Burger, Robert 65, 94
Burns, George 48, 70
Burton, Richard 5, 73
Byrne, David 81
Callas, Maria 71
Campbell's Soup Can 2
Capote, Truman 60
Carson, Johnny 104, 105
Cartland, Barbara 54
Celebrity Squares 24
Cemmick, Paul 92
Chandler, Raymond 54
Charles, Ray 108
Cherry, Jim 82
Child, Julia 25, 45
Ching, Chiang 107
Claus, Santa 62
Cleese, John 16
Cliff, Jimmy 35
Clinton, George 43
Collins, Joan 18, 51
Connors, Jimmy 23
Conway, Michael K. 18
Cooder, Ry 35
Cooke, Sam 87
Copeland, Stewart 36
Costello, Elvis 43
Cronkite, Walter 78
Crosby, Stills and Nash 20
Dangerfield, Rodney 33
Daniels, Alan 51
Davis, Bette 12
Davis, Miles 42
Davis, Sammy Jr. 98
Day, Doris 19, 35
deMar, Charles 2
Dean, James 2, 89
Dietrich, Marlene 110
Dilakian, Hovik 8
Dillon, Matt 68
Disney, Walt 107
Divine 19
Dolle, Tom 88
Doud, Mike 18, 105, 107, 112
Dracula 63
Dreyfuss, Richard 57
Dryden, Patricia 37, 74, 81
Duck, Marlene 110
Duck, Raquel 110
Duck, Sophia 111
Duckula 18
Dunaway, Faye 4
Duvall, Robert 5, 50
Dylan, Bob 14, 65
Eastwood, Clint 38
Edinger, Tom 12, 13, 96
Einstein, Albert 56
Ellington, Duke 8
Exene 31
Farrow, Mia 17
Field, Ann 68, 82
Fink, Mike 106
Fonda, Jane 44, 84
Ford, Harrison 38
Foster, Jodie 83
Franklin, Aretha 64
Freed, Alan 65
Freud, Sigmund 104
Funicello, Annette 70
Garbo, Greta 13
Gardner, Ava 59
Garland, Judy 69
Geary, John 50
Geary, Tony 57

Gere, Richard 83
Gibson, Mel 46
Gillespie, Dizzy 8
Glass, Randy 51
Go-Go's, The 30
Godzilla 32
Goethals, Raphaelle 13
Gold, Jeff 23, 47, 68, 85
Green, Al 87
Grossman, Robert 20, 22, 23, 25, 48, 67, 72, 78, 104, 108
Hagen, Nina 26, 30
Haggerty, Mick 1, 13, 18, 19, 21, 39, 107
Hall and Oates 5
Halston 82
Harada, Osamu 60
Harlow, Jean 13, 73
Harper, Tess 5
Harrison, Malcolm 16, 74
Harry, Deborah 64
Hawn, Goldie 12, 83
Hayworth, Rita 12
Heaven, Hell and Rock & Roll 62
Hechter, Daniel 82
Heimann, Jim 79
Hemingway, Mariel 83
Hendrix, Jimi 65
Henry, Buck 16
Henry, James 4, 45, 98
Hepburn, Katharine 4, 44, 59
Herman, Pee-Wee 48, 57
Hernández, Richard 38
Hockney, David 11, 60
Holder, Geoffrey 70
Holiday, Billie 102, 103
Holly, Buddy 42, 64
Hollyhead, Bush 28, 40, 42, 81, 109
Holmes, Nigel 101
Hope, Bob 49
Hudson, Rock 46
Hynde, Chrissie 27
Idol, Billy 99
Irons, Jeremy 50
Irving, John 55
Jackson, Joe 37
Jackson, Michael 94
Jackson, Reggie 22
Jagger, Mick 5, 26, 60, 64, 65, 75, 83
James, Patrick 95
James, Rick 95
Jarreau, Al 9
Jenner, Bruce 22
Joel, Billy 36
John, Elton 94
Jones, Grace 26
Jones, Mick 14
Jones, Quincy 9
Jones, Rickie Lee 31
Jude, Conny 31
Katsu 5, 8, 14, 30, 37, 42, 53, 55, 56, 67, 85, 86
Kaufman, Andy 49
Kawamura, Yosuke 21, 35, 37, 54, 108
Keeler, Ruby 72
Kelemen, Stephen 104
Kelly, Grace 59
Kennedy, Bobby 6
Kennedy, John F. 7, 72
Kenzo 82
Kid Creole and the Coconuts 53
King Kong 33
Kinski, Nastassja 68
Klein, Calvin 83
Kline, Kevin 73
Knock, Peter 106
Konno, Ken 13, 65, 110
Kopecky, Robert 33, 49, 54, 57, 101
Kristofferson, Kris 34
Kurosawa, Akira 67
Lasorda, Tommy 23
Lassie 112
Laurel and Hardy 72
Laverne and Shirley 4
Lee, Bruce 85
Lennon, John 27, 64, 65, 109
Lennox, Annie 27, 30
Leonard, Sugar Ray 23
Letterman, David 79
Levine, Bette 75, 76
Lewis, Jerry 29
Liberace 95
Lichtenstein, Roy 6
Lieberman, Ron 91
Little Miss Marker 41
Lombard, Carole 13
Loren, Sophia 111
Lowe, Rob 68
M*A*S*H 93
Mahon, Rich 9, 31, 102
Mailer, Norman 18
Mansfield, Jayne 13, 34
Marley, Bob 81, 108
Marsh, Cynthia 2, 4, 9, 18, 26, 27, 30, 56, 92, 98, 105, 107, 112
Marx, Groucho 5, 48
Masi, George 10
Mattelson, Marvin 7, 11, 22, 55, 104
Mayfield, Curtis 87
McCartney, Paul 35
McDowell, Malcolm 85
Meir, Golda 60
Meisel, Ann 48, 50, 57, 78, 84, 94, 95
Mengers, Sue 78
Merkin, Richard 53, 55
Midler, Bette 3
Miller, Henry 55
Mineo, Sal 78
Mingus, Charles 47
Minnelli, Liza 4, 60
Miranda, Carmen 5
Mitchell, Joni 103
Mitchum, Robert 38
Mondrian, Mickey 107
Monroe, Marilyn 40, 76-77

Moon, Keith 109
Moore, Dudley 50
Moroder, Giorgio 79
Morrison, Jim 14
Mouse, Minkey 106
Mr. "T" 33
Mummy, Mickey 106
Murphy, Eddie 49
Nagai, Hiroshi 37, 87, 108
Nelson, Willie 14
Nessim, Barbara 103
Nevelson, Louise 11
Newman, Paul 69
Nicholson, Jack 4
Nicks, Stevie 102
Nixon, Richard 72
Novak, Kim 59
O'Hara, Maureen 97
Olinsky, Frank 81
Onassis, Jackie Kennedy 79
Oreos, The 52
Orwell, George 2
Osto, Ben 45, 49, 62, 98, 101
Our Gang 88
Panter, Gary 13, 33, 48, 89
Park, Neon 18, 110, 111
Parton, Dolly 34
Peck, Everett 5, 48, 67, 85, 92, 106
Perelman, S.J. 55
Petty, Tom 37
Piercy, Clive 2, 89
Police, The 20, 21
Pop Boys, The 61
Pop, Iggy 14
Powell, Dick 72
Powell, William 73
Presley, Elvis 2, 26, 57, 64, 80, 90-91
Prince 35
Pryor, Richard 14
Queen Elizabeth 106
Radner, Gilda 44
Rampling, Charlotte 51
Reagan, Ronald 1, 89, 100-101
Reagans, The 4
Redding, Otis 37
Redford, Robert 34
Reed, Lou 81
Reott, Paul 10
Reynolds, Burt 34
Richards, Keith 5, 14
Risko, Robert 4, 5, 12, 17, 22, 42, 44, 45, 51, 57, 70, 76, 79, 100, 102, 104
Rivera, Chita 4
Rivers, Joan 70, 84, 104
Rolling Stones, The 14
Rosenwald, Laurie 40, 81
Ross, Diana 102
Royal Family, The 92
Ruddell, Gary 63
Rundgren, Todd 35
Sagan, Carl 10
St. Laurent, Yves 82
Salvati, Jim 36, 108
Sarandon, Susan 51
Sato, Pater 46, 53
Scheib, Earl 89
Schorr, Kathy Staico 16, 38, 99
Schorr, Todd 29, 32
Schroder, Ricky 56
Schwarzenegger, Arnold 70
Sedgwick, Edie 88
Selleck, Tom 50
Setzer, Brian 78
Shakespeare, William 10
Shannon, Craig 31, 33, 43, 107, 109
Shepard, Sam 54
Shields, Brooke 68
Sinatra, Frank 19, 43, 98
Sixties, The 92
Smith, Kate 44
Smith, Laura 8, 73
Smith, Patti 14
Soderlind, Kirsten 5, 10, 78
Spago 93
Sparacio, Mark 73
Spielberg, Steven 67
Springfield, Rick 4, 94
Springsteen, Bruce 64
Stallone, Sylvester 85
Stewart, Rod 5, 74
Sting 27, 36
Stray Cats 53
Streep, Meryl 13, 73
Streisand, Barbra 45
Sunset Blvd. 73
Swanson, Gloria 70
Taggart, Nick 26, 27, 73, 93
Tankersley, Paul 5, 44, 88
Taylor, Elizabeth 5, 58, 69, 73
Tex, Joe 87
Tierney, Gene 58
Tomita, Tom 38, 69
Tomlin, Lily 29
Tosh, Peter 108
Townshend, Pete 36
Tracy, Spencer 4
Travolta, John 40
Trudeau, Margaret 92
Tsuchihashi, Kyoko 11, 19, 30
Tune, Tommy 5
Twiggy 5
Ullmann, Liv 51
Vartan 40
Voo, Rhonda 72, 102, 103
Vreeland, Diana 82
Waits, Tom 61
Wall, Pam 75, 94
Warhol, Andy 11, 56, 60
Warhol, Andy 2, 60, 77, 82
Watts, Stan 9, 93
Weatherhead, Mark 34, 73, 98, 103, 111
Weaver, Earl 22
Welch, Raquel 110

Welk, Lawrence 98
Welles, Awesome 29
West, Nathanael 79
Wexler, Ed 29, 52, 65, 79, 100, 101
Whitesides, Kim 5, 10, 20, 23, 31, 36, 43, 44, 50, 62, 69, 90
Willardson, David 16, 64, 90, 94
Williams, Esther 84
Williams, Hank 94
Williams, Wendy O 53
Williams, Robin 48
Wilson, Rob 65, 109
Winwood, Stevie 35
Wolfe, Tom 10
Wolfman 63
Wonder, Stevie 64
Wood, Natalie 34
Woollcott, Alexander 10
Wright, Ian 64
Yamaguchi, Harumi 17, 51, 58-59, 97, 110
Yamura, Tara 79
Yellow Magic Orchestra 21
Yokoo, Tadanori 20, 76
Young, Neil 37
Zadora, Pia 45
Zick, Brian 63
Ziemienski, Dennis 44

Lassie Cynthia Marsh, Mike Doud

Acknowledgments

I would like to thank the following for their cooperation and assistance:

GP Color/Cathy Lynch
Andresen Typographics
Stat House
Wilcopy
NTA Studios, London
Andy Warhol, Fred Hughes/Factory, N.Y.C.
Hiroko Tanaka/Illustration Magazine, Tokyo
Parco Publishing Co./Tokyo
Craig Butler/Workbook, L.A.
Ian Shipley Books Ltd., London
First Impressions, Toronto
Castelli Gallery, N.Y.C./Mary Jo, John Good
Rudy Hoglund, Nigel Holmes/Time Magazine
TV Guide
Interview Magazine
People Magazine
Time Magazine
Playboy Magazine
Rolling Stone Magazine
Penthouse Magazine
Playgirl Magazine
New York Magazine
California Magazine
Los Angeles Magazine
Esquire Magazine
GQ Magazine
Art Direction Magazine

Mom and Dad
Sarah Jane Freymann
Bette Midler
Jerry Blatt
Bonnie Martel
Teri and Brooke Shields
Michael Jackson
Mike Fink
Richard Bernstein
Mary Ann Fujii
Kyoko Tsuchihashi
Michael Hodgson
Lloyd Ziff
Les Mintz
Elyse Rosenthal
Jack and Joan Quinn
Joan Love Allemand
Jon Sher
Robert Fitch/Paper Moon
Genine and Debbie
Fred and Linda
Jean and Bill
Bill, Russ and Martin
American Showcase:
Beth, Fiona, Chris and Ira

Paintings by Andy Warhol courtesy of Leo Castelli Gallery, N.Y.C.

Bobby Kennedy, cover of Time Magazine ® 1968, Time, Inc. All Rights Reserved.

With much respect to the memory of Patrick Nagel.

Any omission of credit is inadvertent and will be corrected in future printings if notification is sent to the publisher.